animals**animals**

Cranes and Storks

by **Steven Otfinoski**

mc **Marshall Cavendish**
Benchmark
New York

Thanks to Donald E. Moore III, associate director of animal care at the Smithsonian Institution's National Zoo,
for his expert reading of this manuscript.

Marshall Cavendish Benchmark
99 White Plains Road
Tarrytown, New York 10591-5502
www.marshallcavendish.us

Library of Congress Cataloging-in-Publication Data

Otfinoski, Steven.
Cranes and Storks / by Steven Otfinoski.
p. cm. — (Animals animals)
Includes index.
Summary: "Provides comprehensive information on the anatomy, special
skills, habitats, and diet of cranes and storks"—Provided by publisher.
ISBN 978-0-7614-3973-8
1. Storks—Juvenile literature. 2. Cranes (Birds)—Juvenile literature.
I. Title.
QL696.C535O84 2009
598.3'2—dc22
2008020913

Photo research by Joan Meisel

Cover photo: Tom Vezo/Minden Pictures

The photographs in this book are used by permission and through the courtesy of:
AP Images: 38, 39. Alamy: franzfoto.com, 10, 32; Arco Images GmbH, 11; Gary Dublanko, 14.
Animals Animals - Earth Scenes: Studio Carlo Dani, 27; Mark J. Barrett, 36. Corbis: Theo Allofs, 1; Arthur Morris, 4, 33;
Steve & Ann Toon/Robert Harding World Imagery, 6; Franz Lanting, 22; Uwe Walz, 30; Raymond Gehman, 34;
Jeff Vanuga, 37. Getty Images: Roy Rainford, 7; altrendo images, 8; Panoramic Images, 12; DAJ, 17;
Heinrich van den Berg, 28. Minden Pictures: Winfried Wisniewski, 18; Tim Fitzharris, 20; David Pike, npl, 23;
Barry Mansell, 25. Peter Arnold Inc.: Biosphoto/Denis-Huot Michel & Christine, 16.
Photo Researchers, Inc.: Millard H. Sharp, 9.

Editor: Joy Bean
Publisher: Michelle Bisson
Art Director: Anahid Hamparian
Series Designer: Adam Mietlowski

Printed in Malaysia
1 3 5 6 4 2

Contents

Beauty on the Wing

On land or in the air, few birds are as graceful as storks and cranes. These tall birds have fascinated people for centuries. They are characters in folklore, legend, and myth. Many peoples consider them a sign of good fortune. And people around the world tell the story of the stork bringing human babies to lucky couples. Of course storks do not really deliver babies to couples. This legend probably began because storks (and cranes, too) are such loving parents to their own babies.

Storks and cranes are not in the same animal family, but they are often grouped together because they share many physical characteristics. Both storks and

Cranes are well known for being good parents. Here, two crane chicks rest on their mother's back.

cranes are large birds with long and slender legs, long necks, and pointed beaks or *bills*. They are also both *wading birds*. That means they spend much of their time walking in the shallow waters of streams, ponds, and marshes, or in nearby grasslands. Even though storks and cranes both have wings, these birds spend far more time on land and in water than in the air.

Storks and cranes look very similar, but storks have a longer bill than cranes. This is a saddle-billed stork.

Cranes are taller than storks. This is a sandhill crane.

With all things they have in common, you might have a hard time telling a stork and a crane apart. But there are a few differences. Cranes are generally taller than storks, and they have longer necks. Another difference between the two is that storks' bills are longer and heavier than the bills of cranes. Also, cranes fly with their necks outstretched, while storks fly with their necks pulled in.

Species Chart

◆ The white stork is the world's best-known stork. It lives in Europe, Asia, and Africa. It stands 3 feet (1 meter) tall and is white in color with black markings on its wings. It has a red beak and reddish-pink legs and feet. The white stork migrates to central Africa and northern India in the winter.

A white stork.

A wood stork adult and chick.

◆ The wood stork is the only stork native to the United States. It is 4 feet (1.2 m) tall and has a *wingspan* of 5.5 feet (1.7 m). It weighs about 4.5 to 5.8 pounds (2 to 2.6 kilograms). The wood stork is white with black markings on its wings and tail feathers. It lives in the swamps of Florida and Georgia, as well as the coastal areas of Central and South America.

◆ The whooping crane is the tallest bird in North America. It stands up to 5 feet (1.5 m) tall and has a wingspan of 6 to 7 feet (1.8 to 2.1 m). It weighs 13.3 to 17 pounds (6 to 7.7 kg). The whooping crane is white with black feathers on its wing tips. It has red skin on its forehead and cheeks. It lives most of the year in northern Canada and flies to Texas's Gulf Coast in the winter.

A whooping crane.

A black crowned crane.

◆ The black crowned crane is named for its colorful yellow crest—or feathers atop its head—and its black body. It is 3 feet (1 m) tall and has a wingspan of 6 to 7 feet (1.8 to 2.1 m). It weighs about 8.5 pounds (3.8 kg). The female has a smaller crest than the male. The black crowned crane lives in northeast and northwest Africa.

One of the easiest ways to tell cranes and storks apart is to listen to them. The crane has a loud voice and its noises can be heard up to a mile away. The stork, on the other hand, cannot vocalize. The only noise it makes is when it communicates with other birds by clattering its bill.

There are nineteen *species*, or kinds, of storks. Sixteen of them live in the Eastern Hemisphere. Just three of the species live in the Western Hemisphere, which includes North and South America. There are

Did You Know . . .
The black crowned crane and its cousin, the grey crowned crane, are the only cranes that make their nests in trees.

A stork takes flight above a field.

fifteen species of cranes. Thirteen of them live in Europe, Africa, and Asia. Only two species live in North America.

All storks have partially webbed feet with four toes. Cranes have three toes on each foot. Both birds' long, thin legs are perfect for wading in water. Their pointed beaks are designed to catch or spear fish and other animals in the water.

When these birds take to the air in flight, it is a spectacular sight. They seem to barely flap their long, spreading wings, but they glide through the air almost effortlessly.

2 Avid Eaters

The shallow waters where storks and cranes wade provide them with most of their food. Black storks and wood storks walk around slowly and patiently, looking down into the water for food. Some stir up the water with one foot. This causes fish or other sea creatures to move about.

When the black stork sees a fat frog or a plump fish swimming by, it will stand as still as a statue. When its prey is close enough, the bird moves with lightning speed. It seizes the frog in its long open beak, or spears the fish through its body with its closed beak. Then it swallows its prey whole. Wood storks do the same, but they use their sense of touch,

This yellow-billed stork has caught a large fish in the water.

not sight, to find their prey. Black storks will also eat small birds and mammals, such as field mice.

The African and Asian openbill storks can grab freshwater snails in their bent bill. Then they crush the snail's shell in the bill's gap to get at the soft body that is inside.

Both cranes and storks eat a variety of things. Here, a stork is catching a frog.

This crane is searching for food in the grass with some help from its young.

Cranes and storks are *omnivores* and will eat plants as well as animals and fish. They also like to eat berries, acorns, and fruits. Some storks, such as marabous, which are the largest storks, will even eat dead animals they find. These storks serve a good purpose by keeping the environment clean and stopping the spread of disease from dead animals.

A crane's size will often determine the kind of food it favors. Short-billed cranes will graze on grass on solid ground and dig around for insects. Longer-billed cranes will hunt for shellfish in shallow waters. The biggest cranes have huge, powerful bills they use to dig up roots to eat in wetlands.

Many storks and cranes are *migratory* birds. In the winter they travel to warmer places where they can find food. Whooping cranes live most of the year in

Did You Know . . .
Stork chicks can eat up to 60 percent of their own body weight each day. If you weigh 80 pounds (36 kg), that would be like eating 48 pounds (22 kg) of food every day.

This flock of sandhill cranes is landing in a field during migration.

northern Canada, but in the winter they travel several thousands miles to the Gulf of Mexico near Texas. During the long flight, the cranes call to each other with loud bugle-like noises. That is how they got the name "whooping cranes." Scientists think they whoop to keep track of each other during the long migration south. Once on the warm Gulf Coast, the cranes live on a diet of mostly crabs, clams, and crayfish.

The white stork travels even farther than the whooping crane in its annual migration. It flies from Europe to Africa in the winter. This is a journey of more than 6,000 miles (9,650 kilometers).

3 Faithful Parents

Some people feel a special closeness with storks simply because some of them live so nearby. In Northern Europe, for instance, white storks sometimes build their nests on the roofs of houses, chimneys, walls, and haystacks. The birds also build nests in trees, cliff-ledges, and even on the ground.

Stork nests are among the largest nests in nature. They can be 6 feet (1.8 m) across and as deep as 10 feet (3 m). Once a pair of storks build a nest that big, they do not easily abandon it. Each year, white storks return to the same rooftop nests. Sometimes two or more stork couples nest on the same roof. Most people who share their home with the storks welcome the birds' return in the spring.

A white stork and its chicks sit in their nest on a rooftop.

Storks use sticks and plant stems to make sure the nest is strong. They then line the nest with everything they can find—from grass to feathers to bits of cloth—to make it soft. By the time the nest is ready to be used, the stork couple has mated several times and the female is ready to lay her eggs.

Storks and cranes both build large nests and they need to find a lot a material to build up those nests.

A pair of red-crowned cranes do a courtship dance.

Cranes build their nests in marshes and other wetlands, usually in quiet, hidden places where *predators* will not disturb them or try to eat their eggs. Cranes have a unique way of mating. They begin with a complicated mating dance. The male and female cranes circle each other, keeping their heads low and their wings open. They leap and bound in the air as they circle each other. Scientists do not yet fully understand the meaning of the dance cranes do, or its curious movements.

Female storks lay between two and six eggs in their nests. They lay one egg every two days. Cranes generally lay only two eggs. After mating, most male birds leave the females, never to return. But not male storks and cranes. They are faithful fathers, and they share the work of caring for the eggs. People once thought that storks mated for life and were *monogamous*. After much study, however, scientists now believe that these birds are serially monogamous. This means they often find new mates after a season or migration.

The male and female birds take turns sitting on the eggs. This process of keeping the eggs warm until they are ready to be hatched is called *incubation*. After about thirty-three days, the baby storks and cranes are ready to hatch. Breaking out of the tough eggshell is hard work. The chicks use a hard knob at the tip of their upper bill called an *egg tooth*. This knob helps them break through the shell and emerge from the egg. The egg tooth falls off the chick's bill a day or two after it hatches.

The first weeks of life are difficult for new stork chicks. Cold weather, predators, and lack of food cause several of them to die. The odds are even worse

A stork chick, which just hatched from its shell, sits by as another chick begins to make its way out of its shell.

for the baby cranes. The first chick to emerge from its egg usually becomes the dominant chick. In its fight for survival, it often tries to push the second chick out of the nest, to seize all the food its parents provide, or even to peck the other chick to death. For these reasons, second chicks do not always survive.

Mother and father work together to get food to feed their young. One guards the nest from intruders while the other goes hunting. The parent that hunts brings various insects and earthworms back to the nest. It often holds the food in the *crop* in its neck to soften it up before feeding it to the chicks.

At about two months, the stork chicks are ready to learn how to fly. Now they are called *fledglings*. By August, white stork fledglings are confident fliers and are ready to start on the long flight from Europe to their winter home in Africa. They fly off in a large group. The parents see them off and stay behind to rebuild the nest for the following year. A month later, the parents are ready to join the migration south and they eventually meet up with their young.

Did You Know . . .
One Siberian crane in *captivity* lived to age eighty-three. He even fathered chicks at the age of seventy-eight.

A white stork feeds its hatchlings.

Most cranes fly south with their young. They stay together and then fly back north in the spring. Only when the next breeding reasons starts will the young birds go off on their own.

Both storks and cranes live for an average of twenty-four years in the wild. In captivity, they can live much longer.

4 Long-distance Fliers

Storks and cranes have few predators in nature. If attacked by another animal, their long, pointed bills are powerful weapons. They use them to stab or bite an enemy.

A more serious threat to the survival of these birds is their long yearly flights to and from their winter homes. If they cannot find suitable resting places along the migratory route, the birds risk dying of exhaustion, hunger, or attacks by predators. Even with enough places to rest, however, the long flights are extremely tiring. The birds' large wings make the flight easier. Stork and cranes have also learned how to conserve their energy over these long distances.

A large, strong bill help storks and cranes protect themselves against predators.

This stork is gliding on a warm air updraft. Gliding helps the stork save energy while flying.

Heat rises and causes *thermal updrafts* in the earth's atmosphere. These powerful movements of warm air can carry flying birds through the air with little effort on their part. Thermal updrafts over bodies of water are very rare, so storks and cranes make their long journeys over land whenever possible. Storks glide on the warm air with their wings outspread. Cranes tend to flap their wings slowly, which helps them conserve energy. With the help of thermal updrafts, these large birds can travel as much as 500 miles (about 800 km) in a single day. The birds must also stop a number of times along the route to rest and to eat. These migratory journeys usually take as long as eight to fifteen weeks to complete.

Whooping cranes, unlike many other cranes and storks, migrate in small family groups instead of large flocks. The group is made up of a mother, a father, and their young. The cranes leave their summer homes in Canada and head south for Texas in September, when the weather grows cold. The adult cranes can travel up to 200 miles (322 km) in a single day without stopping.

Did You Know . . .
A crane can reach flying speeds of up to 70 miles (113 km) per hour.

The young cranes are not strong enough to travel that far without frequent rest stops so the family makes stopovers in shallow waterways or flat, open land. Here, they can easily spot approaching predators. They may stay there for just one day or several days while resting or waiting for better flying weather.

The whooping cranes arrive on the Texas Gulf coast in late November or early December. They will live there through the winter and return north in April. By then, the young cranes are strong enough to

Whooping cranes travel very long distances when they migrate.

These young sandhill crane chicks are not ready to migrate yet, but they will be ready soon.

fly on their own without mom and dad looking out for them. They often will travel with a fellow crane their own age.

White storks traveling from western Europe to Africa rest at special stopping places, called staging areas, in countries such as Spain, Hungary, Turkey, Israel, and Egypt. People in these countries recognize the importance of the stopping places and have worked to preserve these natural spots for the birds. If the staging areas were destroyed by human development, the birds would have fewer places to rest and to eat.

But this is just one threat that storks and cranes face today. People have created most of these threats, and people are the only ones who can end them.

Storks, Cranes, and People

People in many cultures believe that storks and cranes bring them good fortune. Recently, though, people have brought much misfortune to these graceful birds.

Most storks and cranes live in wetlands, but these unique areas are rapidly shrinking. Over time, people have drained more and more swamps and marshes to use the land for farming, homes, and businesses. Storks and cranes have lost not only much of their *habitat*, but also their food source. The frogs, reptiles and fish they eat have disappeared with the destruction of their own habitat.

Storks that live in the woods have suffered, too. Many of the nesting trees of the wood stork of North

This wood stork lives in Florida's Corkscrew Swamp Sanctuary.

America have been chopped down to make way for buildings and roads. When the wood stork was close to becoming *extinct,* the National Audubon Society created a wild bird *preserve.* In 1952 the society established the Corkscrew Swamp Sanctuary in Naples, Florida. In the preserve, wood storks and other endangered birds can nest and live in safety.

The wood stork is not the only wading bird that is *endangered* in North America. The whooping crane was once a common sight on the prairies of the United States and Canada. But as settlers moved west

Many storks and cranes live in marshlands. They have been losing their homes to developers who build houses or stores on the land they use as their home.

The wood stork is one of the animals on the endangered species list.

in the mid-1800s, they destroyed the cranes' nesting grounds, and the birds began to die out. By 1941, there were only fifteen whooping cranes left. The species was on the brink of extinction.

Then, in 1971, the U.S. government declared the whooping crane endangered. Congress passed laws to protect the species. This bird was one of the first endangered

Did You Know . . .
The whooping crane has become the symbol of conservation in North America. In 1957, a pair of whooping cranes and their two chicks appeared on a U.S. postal stamp, representing wildlife conservation.

animals to be so protected in the United States. By 2007, the number of whooping cranes living in the wild had increased to 340, and another 145 lived in captivity in zoos and preserves.

More recently, the white stork of Europe and Africa has been threatened. The skies are not as friendly as they once were for these migratory storks. Many storks have accidentally been killed by running

When this stork was left without parents, human helpers took over. They feed and care for the bird in place of the parents.

into electric power lines and factory smokestacks that people have built along the birds' traditional routes.

Some people whose roofs are home to storks have taken an active role in saving the white stork. If one stork parent dies and the other must go in search of food, the people watch over the eggs in their nest. Some human helpers even keep the eggs warm in a special mechanical incubator. Organizations have set up special stork stations to care for and raise young storks that have lost both parents.

Efforts to save storks and cranes are happening around the world. In Asia, several nations have banded together to create special centers, where cranes are bred, raised, and then sent back into the wild.

Hopefully, the future will be bright for these graceful birds of land, water, and sky.

Glossary

bill—The beak of a bird.

captivity—The condition of being kept by people rather than living in the wild.

crop—A pouch in a bird's throat where food is stored.

egg tooth—A hard knob on the end of a chick's bill that it uses to break out of its shell.

endangered— Threatened with extinction.

extinct—No longer existing.

fledglings—Young birds that are learning to fly.

habitat—The place where an animal lives, including the living and nonliving things in the environment.

incubation—The process of keeping eggs warm so that they will hatch.

migratory—Moving from one region to another for feeding and breeding.

monogamous—Having only one mate.

omnivore—An animal that eats both plants and other animals.

predator—An animal that captures and eats other animals to survive.

preserve—A special area set aside for the protection of the plants and animals living there.

prey—An animal that is hunted and eaten by other animals.

species—Groups of animals that share the same characteristics and mate only with their own kind.

thermal updrafts—Natural events in which warm air rises and provides an easy area for birds to fly.

wading birds—Long-legged birds that walk through shallow waters to feed on prey.

wetlands—Land areas that have wet soil, such as marshes and swamps.

wingspan—The length of a bird's outspread wings measured from wingtip to wingtip.

Find Out More

Books

Goodman, Susan E. *Saving the Whooping Crane.* Minneapolis, MN: Millbrook Press, 2007.

Imbriaco, Alison. *The Whooping Crane: Help Save This Endangered Species!* Myreportlinks.com, 2006.

World Book. *Storks and Other Large Wading Birds.* Chicago: World Book, 2005.

Web Sites

Animal Bytes: San Diego Zoo
http://www.sandiegozoo.org/
animalbytes/t-crane.html

International Crane Foundation
http://www.savingcranes.org/

Stork Facts and Photographs
http://montereybay.com/
creagrus/storks.html

Index

Page numbers for illustrations are in **boldface**.

About the Author

Steven Otfinoski is the author of numerous books about animals. He has written *Koalas, Sea Horses, Alligators,* and *Hummingbirds* in the Animals Animals series. Otfinoski lives in Connecticut with his wife, a high school teacher and editor.